In this coloring book you will
find more than 30
exciting shapes and
colors to discover

Enjoy and have fun

THIS BOOK BELONGS TO:

............................

# SQUARE

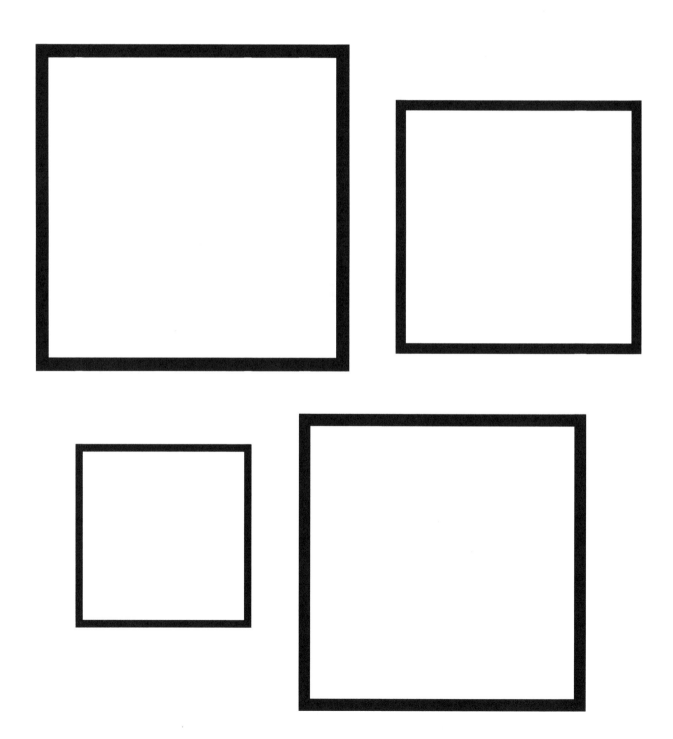

# CIRCLE

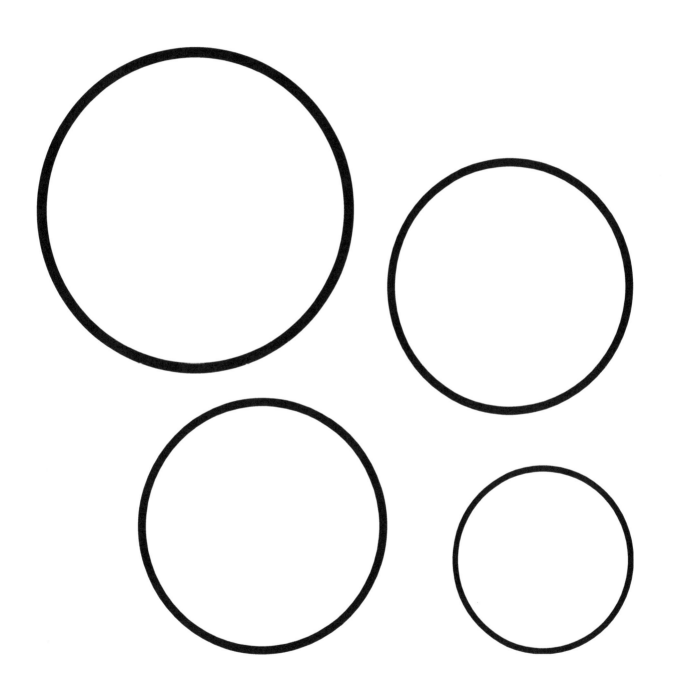

# TRIANGLE

# RIGHT TRIANGLE

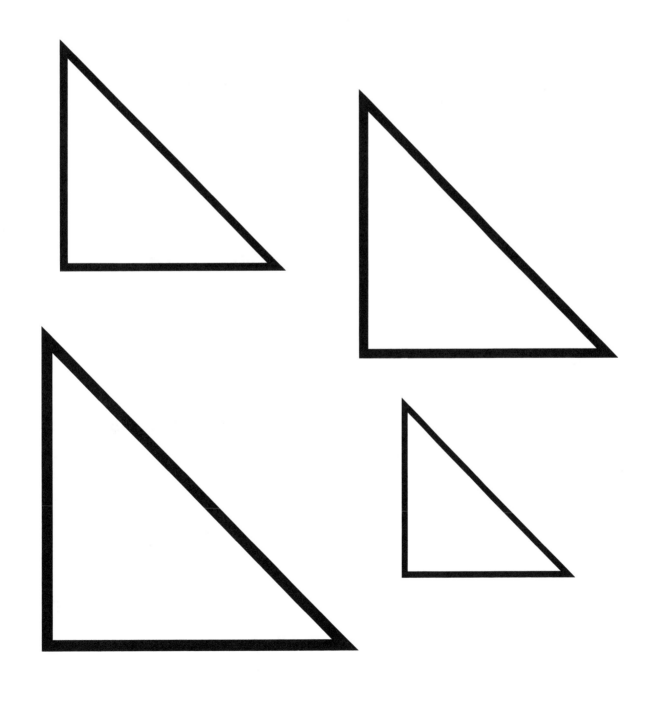

# RECTANGLE

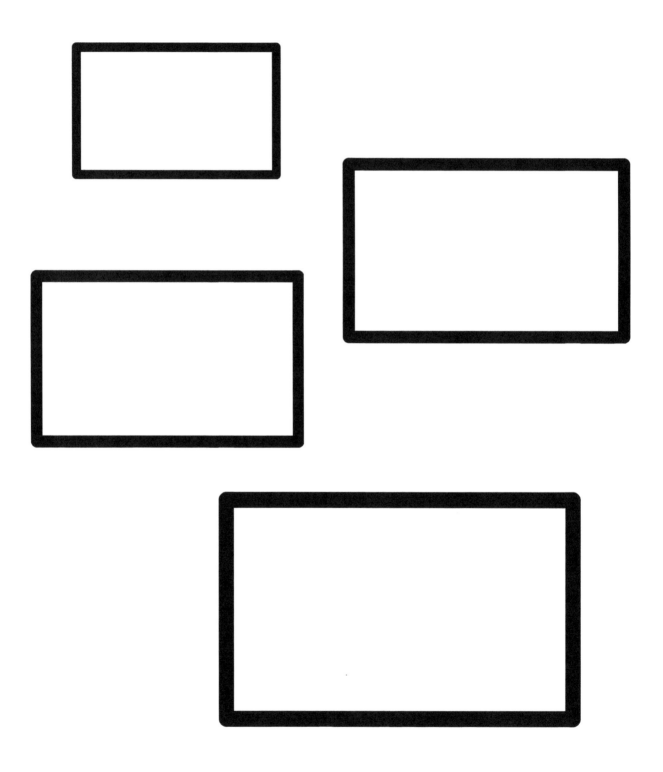

# RHOMBUS

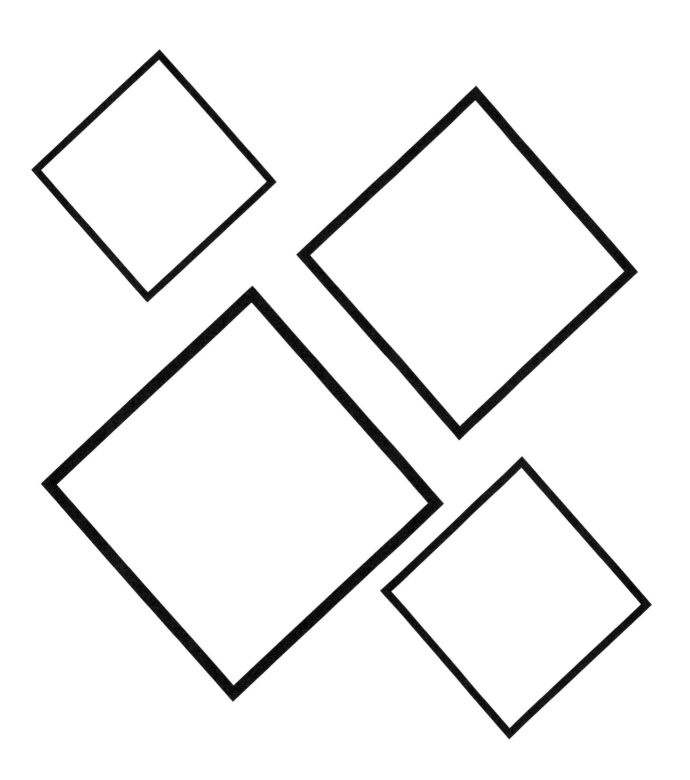

# TRAPEZE

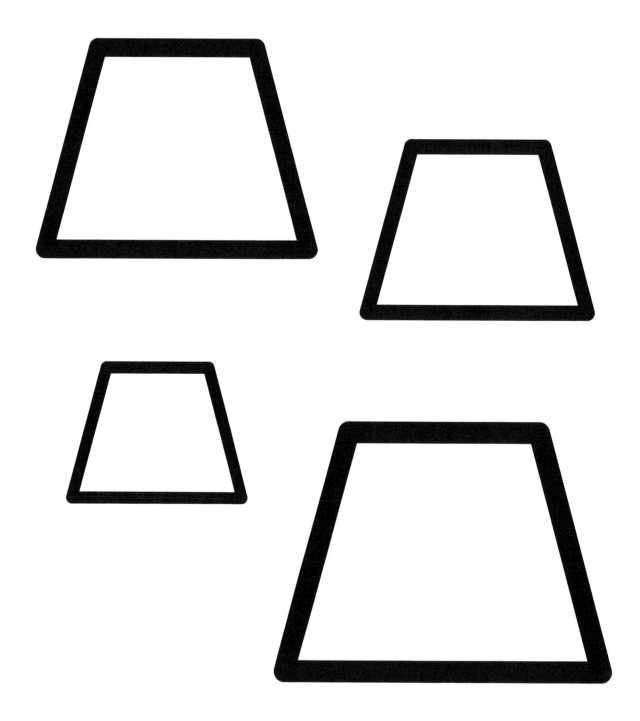

# PENTAGON

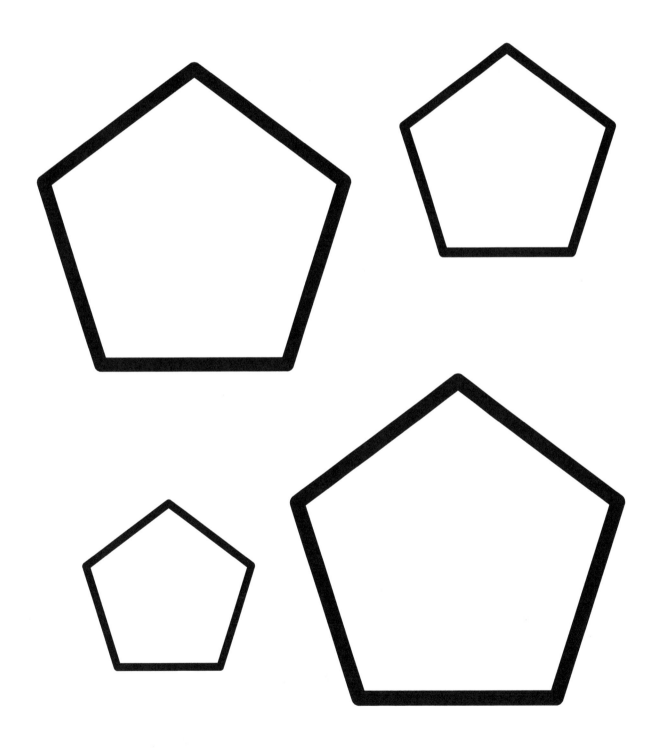

# HEXAGON

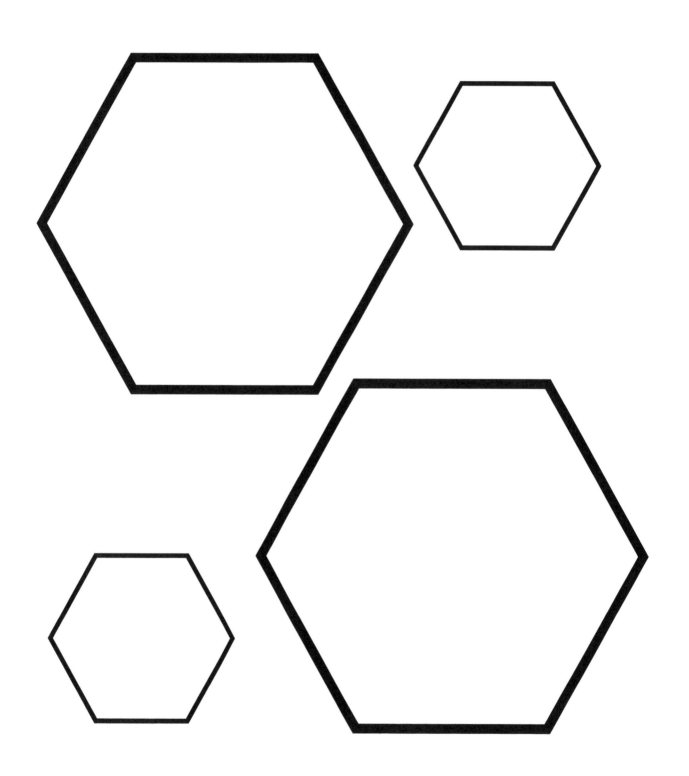

# OCTAGON

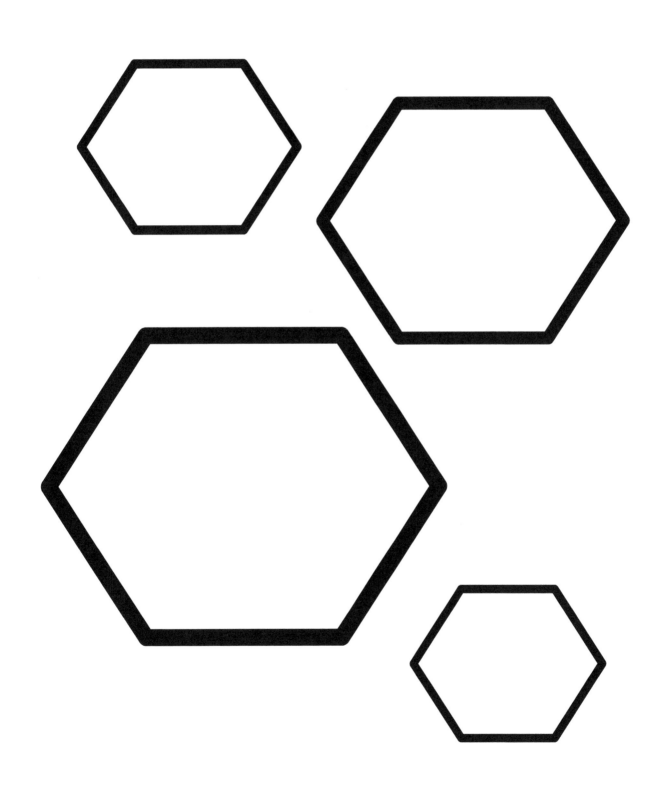

# STAR

# HEART

# ARROW

# CROSS

# CRESCENT

# FIND SHAPES ○ ☆ △

**FIND SHAPES**

**FIND SHAPES**

# FIND SHAPES

# FIND SHAPES

# FIND SHAPES

# FIND SHAPES

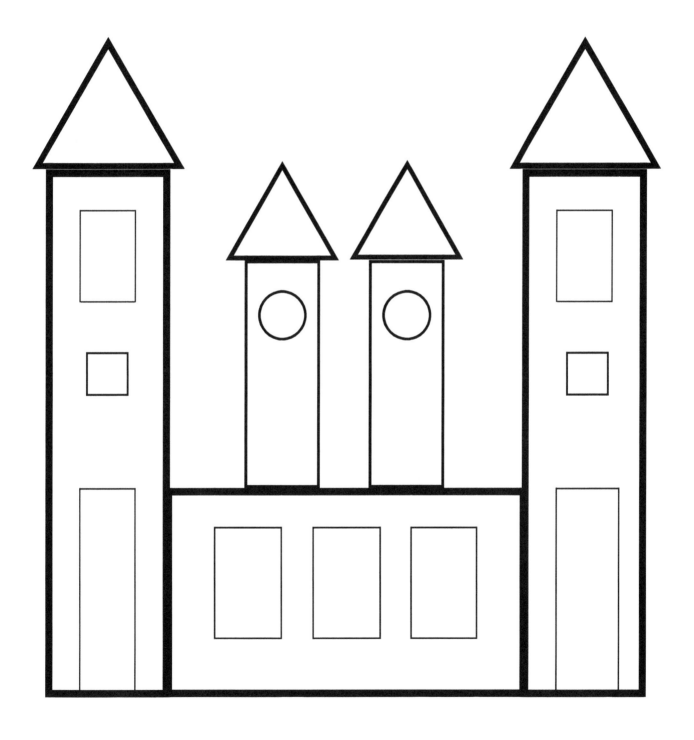

**FIND SHAPES**

# FIND SHAPES

# FIND SHAPES

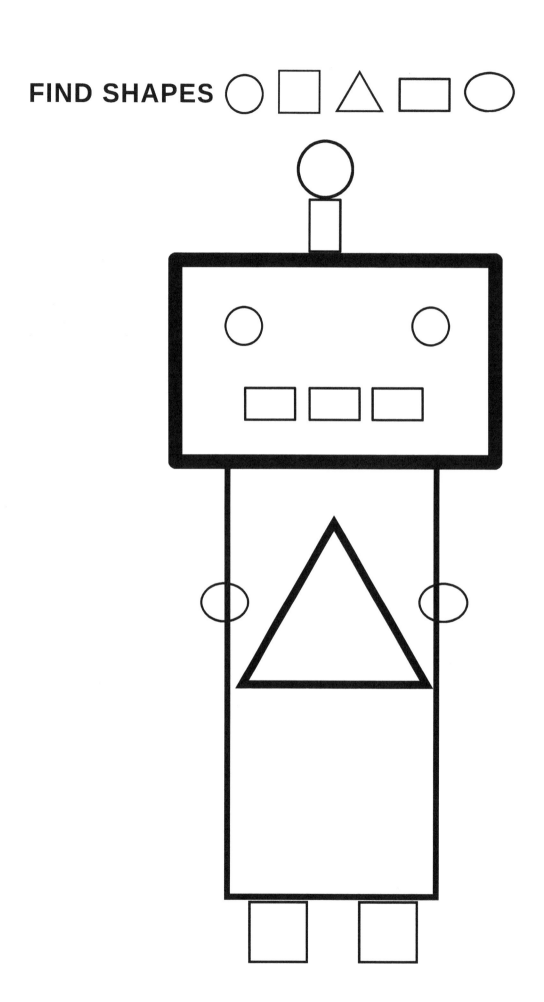

# FIND SHAPES

# FIND SHAPES

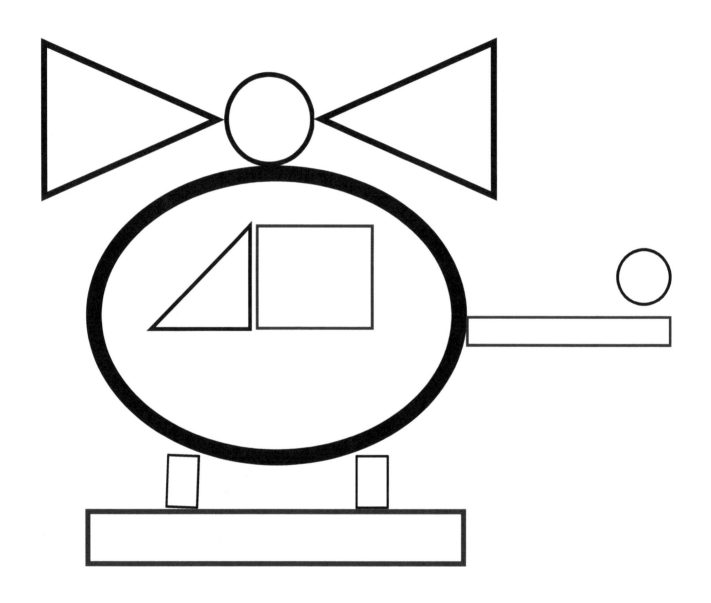

# FIND SHAPES

# RED

# BLUE

# YELLOW

# PINK

# PURPLE

# BROWN

# WHITE

# GREEN

# BLACK

# ORANGE

# GREY

Printed in the USA
CPSIA information can be obtained
at www.ICGtesting.com
LVHW080349131123
763757LV00034B/614